THE FETISH CARVERS

OF ZUNI

Figure 1. Cliff with petroglyphs and pictographs overlooking the ruins of the Village of the Great Kivas, an Anasazi site of the Pueblo II period on the Zuni Reservation.

THE FETISH CARVERS
OF ZUNI

MARIAN RODEE   JAMES OSTLER

PHOTOGRAPHS BY MICHAEL MOUCHETTE

The Maxwell Museum of Anthropology
The University of New Mexico
Albuquerque, New Mexico

The Pueblo of Zuni Arts and Crafts
Zuni, New Mexico

Photography by Michael Mouchette. Designed by Joyce S.
Rhodes and Sheila Edwards, Publications Office, Public
Affairs Department, The University of New Mexico.

Printed in Albuquerque by Starline Printing.

Distributed by The Maxwell Museum of Anthropology, The
University of New Mexico, Albuquerque, NM 87131-1201.

Library of Congress Catalog Number: 90-63002

ISBN 0-912535-05-9

Cover photograph: Dan Poncho holding unfinished fetish.
Preceeding page: Serpentine lizard, Kent Banteah,
3 3/4" long.

We undertook this study because of the great interest in the collecting of fetishes in the 1980s and the concomitant growth in the number of carvers. James Ostler, who established the Pueblo of Zuni Arts and Crafts enterprise in 1984, has been associated with the carving phenomenon from the beginning and has lived at Zuni as both an outsider and an insider. Marian Rodee, curator of Southwestern Ethnology at the Maxwell Museum of the University of New Mexico, approaches the project as a museum person interested in the history and social basis of the native arts of the Southwest. The interviews were conducted in 1988 and 1989 and the photography was done between October 1989 and May 1990.

Many thanks are given to the National Endowment for the Arts Folk Art Program, which funded the traveling exhibition and a portion of this book, and to the New Mexico Endowment for the Humanities, which provided support for the initial travel to Zuni to conduct the interviews and do the planning. Most particularly, we wish to thank Michael Mouchette, University of New Mexico photographer, who took all the shots in this book, and even climbed up the mesa wall at the Village of the Great Kivas packing forty pounds of camera equipment to get photos showing the great antiquity of Zuni carving. We are also grateful to

6

the book designer, Joyce S. Rhodes, and her assistant, Sheila Edwards, and to Catherine Baudoin, Maxwell Museum Store Manager, for her help and encouragement, financial and moral.

At Zuni we would like to thank Pesancio Lasiloo, Lt. Governor; Bill Tsikewa, Councilman and carver; Milford Nahohai for leading us over rooftops to get the best views of the old village of Halona:wa; the staff of Pueblo of Zuni Arts and Crafts, especially Paula Martza, Darcy Dishta and Carla Lahala, who always had an eye out for new fetishes and information about the carvers; and Mary Ghahate for keeping track of all expenses. Thanks go to dealers Don Sharp, Alice Killackey, Pat and Helen Harrington, Corilee Heinis and John Kennedy. We also appreciate the help of our colleagues at other museums, Diana Pardue at the Heard Museum, Louise Stiver at the Laboratory of Anthropology, Steve Rogers of the Wheelwright Museum and Felicia Pickering of the Anthropology Department of the Smithsonian Institution. Unless otherwise noted all fetishes belong to the Pueblo of Zuni.

Most important of all, thanks to the carvers and their families, who patiently answered our questions. Not every artist wished to be interviewed or photographed for this book, and the fact that a carver is not included is his or her choice and not a reflection of the quality of his or her work.

Figure 2. View across the old village of Zuni (Halona:wa).

TABLE OF CONTENTS

Figure 3. Dowa Yalanne
or Corn Mountain.

The village of Zuni lies one hundred and fifty miles west of the Rio Grande Valley on the border of Arizona and New Mexico. Although its language is unique, with no known relatives on the North American continent (Woodbury 1979, 468), its culture is similar to that of other Pueblo groups. All modern Pueblo societies are derived from the prehistoric Anasazi and Mogollon cultures of New Mexico and Arizona. There are tens of thousands of sites dating from 200 B.C. to the present in the Zuni area (Kintigh 1985, 1).

The first direct European contact with the Zunis occurred about 1539 as the result of stories told by two men, Cabeza de Vaca and the Moor, Esteban, both survivors of a shipwreck off the Florida coast in 1528 (Woodbury 1979, 469-471). For ten years the two men wandered throughout what is now the southern and southwestern United States. When they finally reached the Spanish provincial capital in Mexico City, they told wondrous tales of the fabulously rich Seven Cities of Cibola to the north. A small party led by Father Marcos de Niza and Esteban visited Zuni in 1539. Esteban went ahead into the village and was killed by the Zunis, supposedly because of his arrogant behavior. Some members of Esteban's party made it back to Father Marcos de Niza, who then went home with reports that only increased the appetite of the Spaniards to explore the northern frontier.

A large, well-armed expedition led by Francisco Coronado and accompanied by Father Marcos de Niza visited Zuni in 1540. A battle ensued between Coronado and the Zunis at the southern village of Hawikuh. Though wounded, Coronado was able to enter the village with his troops, and the Zunis sued for peace. A mission was established in 1630 and soldiers were garrisoned at Hawikuh, but no Spanish civilians lived in the Zuni area until the late nineteenth century. The Zunis, aligned with other Indian pueblos, succeeded in ejecting all the Spanish in the Pueblo Rebellion of 1680. At this time the Zunis abandoned their six villages to move to small, easily defended settlements on top of Dowa Yalanne (Corn Mountain) (Fig. 3). After the Spanish reconquest of 1692, the Zunis settled in the valley again, but this time in one major village with agricultural outliers. In 1990 Zuni is still only one large village with four seasonally occupied farming and ranching communities. Because of the area's remoteness from the seat of Spanish power in Santa Fe and its vulnerability to Navajo and Apache raiding, lands adjacent to Zuni were not settled until the second half of the nineteenth century. Perhaps that accounts for the lesser impact of Spanish culture and religion on the Zunis than on the Indians of many other communities. The Spanish introduced sheep, burros, horses, and wheat, as well as a wide range of new diseases that caused a drastic reduction in the population.

Zuni today is a village of about 9,400 people (Fig. 2). There are 8,996 Zunis on the tribal rolls and approximately 400 non-Zunis.

Figure 4. Looking across the rooftops of Zuni (Halona:wa).

Figure 5. Bread ovens (*hornos*) near the river, belonging to Myrtle Penketewa.

Figure 6. Woodpiles in Zuni (Halona:wa).

Membership in the tribe is decided on the basis of at least one- quarter Zuni blood, and the population is increasing at the rate of about 300 per year (Zuni Census Office, personal communication, 1990). Gallup, New Mexico, is the closest town, and lies thirty-five miles to the north on Interstate 40. Zuni has its own school system, courts, and tribal government, all of which bring in information from the outside world and at the same time act as buffers between individual Zunis and outside laws and standards. The community has preserved its own language, which nearly all Zunis speak, and which is the medium of gossip, banter, traditional practices and home. English is the language of the school and the marketplace.

The village is grouped into two major population areas: the old village of Halona:wa, where all religious events occur, and the "suburb" of Black Rock. There are two food markets, one convenience store, two gas stations, two hardware stores, four cafes, one deli, and seven stores buying and selling arts and crafts. Zuni is served by one hospital, two high schools, two junior high schools, two grade schools, a Head Start preschool, and a branch of a branch of the University of New Mexico.

Zuni also has six kivas, seven medicine societies, seventeen clans, two religious fraternities, and groups of religious clowns. Sporadically pow wow groups and dance troupes perform social dances outside the Pueblo. The rituals of winter continue to be practiced to bring medicine, blessings, peace, harmony, long life, and fertility. The rituals of summer are held to provide rain and good crops. Masked religious dances occur in ongoing cycles performed by the six kivas. There are also numerous parades every year in which Zuni social dance troupes may perform. In the village of 1990 even the outsider can see the kachinas in the night dances and the summer rain dances and sense the jokes, laughter and the proscriptions of the Mudhead Clowns. The outsiders can feel the terror of young and old as the Atoshle, a bogeyman or ogre kachina, makes his rounds. It is the exception for a young boy not to be initiated into a kachina society, and likewise it is the exception for any initiated member not to follow the prescriptions of his or her society or fraternity. Though it is good to get away for short trips, for almost all Zunis there is only one place for a Zuni to live: the old village of Halona:wa, in the center of the Zuni Reservation, a place where their ancestors have lived for at least the last one thousand years.

Zuni is a densely populated, face-to-face village with a highly efficient gossip network. Houses are set close to one another, with extended families often residing in the same or neighboring houses, and there is little that happens that is not commented on. To the outsider, Zuni appears to be a village with its value system intact and with a clear sense of what is Zuni. Outsiders who are allowed to live in Zuni, whether Anglo or from another tribe, are never allowed to forget their place of origin, nor will they, no matter what they do, be incorporated into the tribe. Nonetheless, even the outsider, after just a short absence from Zuni, begins to

Figure 7. The mission church at Zuni with *campo santo* or graveyard in the foreground.

Figure 8. Tami Tsethlikai and Vinton Hooee in traditional dress at Dowa Yalanne.

Figure 9. Pictographs of kachinas at the Village of the Great Kivas.

hunger for its sounds, smells, and gossip.

Traditionally, Zuni political authority was exercised by the religious leaders, who frequently inherited their offices. Now, however, as a result of dealing with the Spanish, Mexican, and American administrations, there are two sets of leaders: the traditional religious ones and the democratically elected tribal officials. Families still reckon kinship in the female line, and often the husband goes to live with his wife and mother-in-law in the traditional way of a matrilineal, matrilocal society. These social patterns are evident in how young people learn the arts and how artists work together. It is the strong kinship at Zuni that binds the extended family as a social and economic unit, and it is the unremitting, pervasive, overlapping, and sometimes coercive ties of the religious system that create areas of cooperation among extended families.

Though there are no clear figures on sources of Zuni income, even a short stay in the village demonstrates the economic importance of the arts to the community. At Zuni the arts are a cottage industry, and there is hardly a household in the village that does not receive a major part of its income from the sale of objects that are typically created at a workbench in the living rooms or a back room. Based on figures at the largest grocery store in town, it is estimated that 50 percent of Zuni family income derives from arts and crafts, with federal and state entitlements a distant second (Roger Thomas, personal communication, 1990).

Although the most widely practiced art

is jewelry, many men and women are also potters, bead workers, painters, and carvers. Since these arts can be practiced in the home, the money brought in makes it possible for people to stay at Zuni with their families and still have a means of support. Thus the arts nourish the community in a material way as well as supporting Zuni identity and sense of unique style.

Figure 10. Banded agate male and female coyote fetish. 2 1/2' long. Stevenson and Cushing Collection. Smithsonian Institution. 73685.

The term fetish has such negative associations that it is used with reluctance in this publication. The term is so pervasive, however, that a change at this point would only be confusing. A fetish is an object, natural or man made, in which a spirit is thought to reside and which can be used to effect either good or evil. Zuni belief, like that of most Native Americans, gives a spiritual nature to all animals and plants. In addition, it is believed that animals have powers that humans do not: animals are stronger, faster, and can fly or burrow underground and thus are creatures to be feared and respected. If a stone or a part of the landscape resembles an animal, such as a mountain that looks like a sleeping bear, or a stone shaped like a frog, then the spirit of that animal may reside in those objects. For an individual to gain access to those powers, the animal spirit must be cultivated, and for this reason Zuni fetishes are fed cornmeal and water, kept in a protected place, and given gifts of turquoise and coral. The bundle tied to fetishes, typically small beads and arrowheads, can be seen as an offering to the animal spirit that resides within and as the fetish is honored or nourished so the animal spirit is nourished through the fetish.

Most of what is written about the significance of fetishes was published by Frank Hamilton Cushing in 1883 (*Zuni Fetiches* in the

Figure 11. Alabaster eagle with stone point tied on with sinew and pierced for suspension. Stevenson and Cushing Collection. Smithsonian Institution. 73651.

Second Annual Report of the Bureau of American Ethnology). So important is this work that it has been reprinted continually since 1966. Cushing was one of three anthropologists sent to Zuni by the Bureau of American Ethnology in Washington, D.C. The other two were James and Matilda Coxe Stevenson. In a total of three expeditions (1879, 1881, and 1884) large collections were made at the Pueblo and sent back to the Smithsonian Institution. The publications of Cushing and the Stevensons provide important information on the life, language, arts and traditional practices of the Zuni people before the changes of the twentieth century (Cushing 1883; Stevenson 1901-02). Cushing not only lived at the Pueblo and learned the language, but was initiated into the Bow Priesthood. Thus, for an outsider, he had unusual insight into Zuni tradition and ceremonialism. The following description of the animals of prey derives from his work.

When the earth was new, the Sun Father sent his own two children to help mankind. Among the many blessings they brought was the destruction of some of the fierce predatory animals that were killing people. The divine children turned the animals to stone with the lightning from their magic shields. Then the children told the animals that by the magic of the heart that remained living within them they were to assist man rather than harm him. This magic refers to the belief that animals of prey charm their quarry into being caught with the breath they exhale from their lungs and hearts as well as their teeth and claws. This belief may shed light on the use of

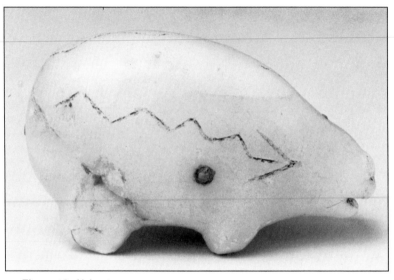

Figure 12. Alabaster bear with incised lines on back and sides filled with red pigment, turquoise between legs. Approximately 6" long. Matilda Coxe Stevenson Collection. Smithsonian Institution. 399125.

the so-called heartline that is inlaid into or painted on the side of fetishes and runs from the mouth to the heart-lungs. A ceremony that honors the spirit of the slain deer may also show the meaning of this line. When a man returns home with a deer, the oldest male member of the hunter's household breathes puffs of tobacco into the nostrils of the dead deer as it lies in state (Ukestine 1989, 5).

The representation of this heart-/ or breathline is extremely rare on early fetishes. The earliest so far noted is one in the collection of the Smithsonian Institution. It is not part of the field collection of fetishes but was willed by Matilda Stevenson to one of her friends who in turn gave it to the museum. The carving, a beautiful, large, white alabaster bear, has a heartline on one side and a plant form on the other (Fig. 12). It is interesting to note that deer, the prey in this case rather than the predator, is shown on late nineteenth century pottery jars with a heartline.

In ancient times the Father of the Medicine Societies, Po-shai-an-kia, established predatory animals as guardians of the six directions. Each of the six directions is associated with a different color: the guardian of the north is the mountain lion and the color is yellow: west, the bear (blue): south, the badger (red): east, the wolf (white): above, the eagle (multicolor), and beneath or at the nadir, the mole (black). The mountain lion is the eldest brother and most important of the directional animals. Their ranking goes counter-sunwise, with the lion followed by the bear, badger, wolf, eagle,

Figure 13. Painted red stone badger with turquoise chips. "Prey animal of the south. Worn about the clothing. Supposed to give them luck while on a hunt of any kind." 3" long. Stevenson and Cushing Collection. Smithsonian Institution. 73684.

Figure 14. Set of fetishes of hunters of the six directions counter-clockwise from the top or north: mountain lion, coyote, wild cat, wolf . Center top: eagle. Bottom: mole. Each about 2" long. Sheche family.

and mole. Po-shai-an-kia charged each animal to protect that region of the Zuni world and to pass messages to him from mankind. Thus these powerful animals are mediators and protectors of the various medicine or healing societies at Zuni. Each of these guardians has a little brother, or counterpart, in each of the other directions.

Animals that protect the hunt are slightly different from the guardians of the directions: the coyote replaces the bear of the west, and the wild cat replaces the badger of the south, but the others remain the same. Carvings of these six animals are the ones carried by Zuni men for a successful hunt. According to legend, when a man finds a rock that resembles an animal, he has in his possession one of the original animals turned to stone by the children of the Sun Father. Such a fetish has the soul or breath of the animal inside and is the most efficacious in hunting. Sometimes such a rock may need some shaping or carving to bring out the full resemblance. All these animals, guardians of the Zuni world and hunting fetishes, are part of the repertoire of modern carvers. The bear is especially popular with the Zuni and the American public and is perhaps the most frequently carved. Bears are known for their healing associations among most Native American groups. Snakes are also important in Zuni ceremonialism, being associated with lightning.

Lizards and, of course, buffalo are also popular local animals and more unusual animals are added all the time. Zunis have an appreciation for nature and all wild creatures and take great pleasure in carving them in stone and shell.

Figure 15. Painted stone mountain lion with two stone points attached with cotton twine. 3 1/4" long. Stevenson and Cushing Collection. Smithsonian Institution. 129118.

Figure 16. Siltstone mountain lion. Head broken off and surface smoothed. Basketmaker III. c.650 A.D. Site south of Sanders, Arizona. A12-B-60-31. Bureau of Indian Affairs. Excavated by Zuni Archaeological Project.

Even in prehistoric times, in addition to natural concretions and other formations resembling predatory animals, there were carved animals (Figs. 16, 17 and 34). The three illustrated here are from sites dating to around A.D. 650 and ancestral to present day Zuni. The ceramic turkey was found in the floor of a great kiva, and the other two were found in storage pits where they may have been placed to protect the food. Although we cannot know what function these prehistoric carvings served, it is reasonable to assume that some of them paralleled the purposes of today's fetishes. For the fetishes collected on the Cushing and Stevenson expeditions, there are no field notes on how the carvings were obtained or from whom. The only notes concern which prey animal is represented and the Zuni name for it. Most of the carvings are of local Zuni stones, often painted to achieve the desired directional color though some are ceramic. They strongly resemble in style the prehistoric carvings. Animals that are carved, rather than purely natural formations, still maintain the feeling of an animal form barely emerging from the raw material. The fetishes are all head and body, the legs are virtually nonexistent, and only those features that are absolutely necessary to identify the animal are shown. Frequently, only slight differences between species are indicated. Thus a thinner, shorter tail and slightly more upright ears differentiate a wildcat from a coyote, and a bushier tail, a wolf from a coyote. Indeed, in the Smithsonian catalogue some of the original identifications were crossed out and "correct-

Figure 17. Ceramic turkey. Found in great kiva. Basketmaker III.c.650 A.D. Site near Tohatchi, New Mexico. LA619.55. Bureau of Indian Affairs. Excavated by Zuni Archaeological Project.

ed." Although traditionally a man would shape his own natural find, there appear to have been semiprofessional carvers supplying fetishes to their families and friends since at least the late nineteenth century. Cushing does not note the existence of fetish carvers, so concerned is he with the ceremonial and mythic aspects, but it is obvious from the evidence of the collection itself that there were specialists at work. Examining photos of a number of Smithsonian carvings they can be divided into several styles, perhaps representing the work of talented individuals or families. The carvings in hematite, a very hard, intractable material are especially well finished and polished (Fig. 21). The older fetishes are as well executed and have the same feeling for the beauty and natural properties of the stone as those made by professional carvers today. This is remarkable when one considers that the nineteenth century carvers were working with simple hand tools and pump drills.

The simple fetish style has continued with little change until the present. Indeed, Zunis have occasionally found prehistoric fetishes in their fields, not surprising since the entire Zuni Valley is filled with archaeological remains. They are picked up and sold to collectors or returned to use. It was not until the early twentieth century that any changes occurred in carving, and they were brought about by the development of Zuni jewelry. When the Zunis learned silversmithing from a Navajo, Atsidi Chon (Ugly Smith), in the late nineteenth century, they followed the old Navajo style of massive pieces with few if any sets. The natural

Figure 18. Painted stone wolf with turquoise eyes and shell point attached with cotton twine. Collected by J.W. Fewkes. 1897. Smithsonian Institution. A176389.

Figure 19. White stone horse with painted features. "Used to hunt strayed horses and carried on long journeys to prevent horses tiring." Stevenson and Cushing Collection. 4 3/4" long. Smithsonian Institution. 73700

Figure 20. Turquoise figure of a Zuni priest with a bowl of "cornmeal". Leekya Deyuse, 1927. 4 3/4" high. Heard Museum. 1707-425.

Figure 21. Hematite lynx or wildcat. 3 1/4"long. Stevenson and Cushing Collection. Smithsonian Institution. 73691.

Figure 22. Shell figure of man in Plains style feather headdress and coral necklace. Leekya Deyuse, 1927. Heard Museum. 1707-448.

Figure 23. Turquoise human hand with red shell nails. Leekya Deyuse, 1930. 4 1/2" long. Heard Museum. 1707-446.

abilities of Zunis for carving stones and a love of turquoise soon led to the development of a distinctive style in which the silver is really a foundation or backdrop for the stones (Adair 1944, 121-36). Silver work was encouraged by trader C. G. Wallace, who came to Zuni in 1918 from North Carolina and quickly saw the potential of jewelry beyond the bounds of the village.

It was talented stone setters such as Teddy Weahkee and Leekya Deyuse who developed a new, more realistic carving style for sale outside of Zuni. John Kennedy, who worked for C. G. Wallace, said that early traders had difficulty selling carvings alone—they had to be mounted on bases or set into jewelry (personal communication, 1989). Most of Leekya's work has survived in jewelry or strung as necklace fetishes, especially his birds (Fig. 26). Many of these early carvings (1920-50) are complete human figures, that is, traditionally dressed Zuni and Navajo men and women: some are just body parts, such as hands and feet, (Fig. 23) or plant forms, especially leaves. The carved hands and feet are intriguing, and their significance is not known, although these extremities are represented prehistorically on pottery and petroglyphs. They may be somewhat influenced by Hispanic *milagros*, the tiny silver body parts that have long been made as votive offerings to the saints for cures.

Until recently, the American public did not collect smallscale Zuni carvings for their own sake. Collectors did appreciate fetish necklaces in the 1960s and 1970s, however, and most of the parents of the present generation of carvers made them. The diminutive animals, already pierced and individually priced, are purchased by dealers and strung according to their own taste or to the order of a particular customer, generally with handmade beads or heishe from Santo Domingo Pueblo (Fig. 50). The Harringtons, traders at Zuni since the early 1960s, believe that all the fetishes made for sale at that time were the small or stringing fetishes and that Rignie Boone was the first Zuni in the 1970s to try again to make larger animal carvings for sale. This statement is contradicted somewhat by Leonard Halate, who says he has been carving table fetishes since at least the 1940s.

It may be, then, that a few carvers were making larger fetishes for sale outside the Pueblo before the 1960s but not in great quantity. In any case, since the 1980s the sale of fetishes has increased dramatically. The marketing conditions at the Pueblo have changed also. Before the Second World War, arts were bartered for credit at the post, but presumably, returning veterans found this system inadequate after experiencing a cash economy. John Kennedy says he was one of the first merchants who gave cash for arts in his store. Moreover, there was very little power equipment at the Pueblo, and most of it was in the hands of traders and used by the men and women in their employ. Twentieth century carving, at least of those pieces intended for sale, is done by both men and women as part of the jewelry process. Thus the development of a market economy, the availability of power equipment,

Figure 24. Turquoise lizard. Teddy Weahkee, 1927. 6 1/2" long. Heard Museum. 1707-426.

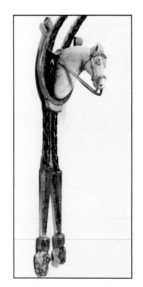

Figure 26. Fossilized ivory horsehead set into bolo tie. Leekya Deyuse, 1935. Heard Museum. 1707-228.

Figure 25. Turquoise figure of a woman carrying a water jar. Leekya Deyuse, 1927. 1 1/2" high. Heard Museum. 1707-448.

and a change in the collecting taste of the American public have all contributed to the creation of modern carving forms and styles.

Figure 27. Ram with turquoise eyes. "Navajo Fetich. Used to secure increase of flocks." Stevenson and Cushing Collection. Smithsonian Institution. 73681.

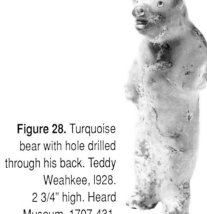

Figure 28. Turquoise bear with hole drilled through his back. Teddy Weahkee, 1928. 2 3/4" high. Heard Museum. 1707-431.

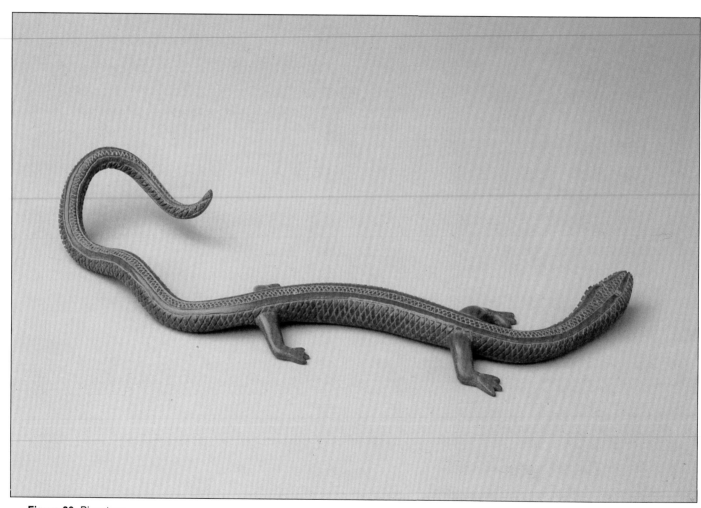

Figure 29. Pipestone
lizard. Darren Shebola.
6 1/2" long.

n 1984 the Pueblo organized the first tribal business to market Zuni arts. When the doors opened in May, the word spread quickly that a new "buyer" was in town, and lines of Zuni craftspeople anxious to sell their work formed across the sales room, out of the door, and along the sidewalk in front of the building. In that first week most of the artists brought in jewelry to sell, but there were also one or two paintings, some small beadwork, and a few fetish carvings. In the first year the tribal business was consistently buying from about a dozen carvers. Serpentine, pipestone, antler, and turquoise were the most common materials used. Fetish carvings were small, generally fitting in the palm of one's hand. Since there were no clear standards of how a fetish carving should look, fetishes were purchased on the basis of what seemed interesting and what could be resold. They were mostly of an older style, generally abstract, and perhaps more crudely carved than later work. More detailed carvings were also available, principally from the Quandelacy and Cheama families.

Of all the crafts at Zuni, jewelry making was the most developed. In 1984, as today, it was essentially a cottage industry in which individual craftspeople or families specialized in the making of a half dozen designs. The craftsperson's small repertoire of designs could then be used to make bolos, pins/pendants, necklaces, rings or earrings as the demand warranted and his buyers requested. Zuni silversmiths feel that designs belong to them: they have either originated them or have inherited them from their parents or an older relative. Not infrequently, a craftsperson admonishes a buyer not to buy from particular people because "they are copying my work." In present-day Zuni, where most of the work in jewelry is done by a husband-and- wife team, even during a short marital separation one spouse may or even his or her family may instruct their buyers not to buy from the estranged party.

Zuni jewelry emphasizes craftsmanship: the tightness of the inlay, the cleanness of the soldering, the delicacy and evenness of the needlepoint, and the high polish of the stones and shell. Since a small repertoire of designs is repeated by each craftsperson, the traders and itinerant buyers quickly learn whom to contact for particular pieces. Even with a thousand craftspeople working daily in the village, there is a predictability in the kinds of jewelry available, and it does not take the trader long to determine what the market price is for a particular bolo or necklace. Since a craftsperson may visit the trader as often as once a week, it also does not take long to know "his price."

In 1984 there was none of this predictability in the fetish market, and hence it was difficult to establish standards for quality and price. At first, purchases were made from only a dozen carvers, but by 1989 the number had grown to 105 active carvers. The variety of ma-

Figure 30. Stone bear. Theodore Kucate, c.1980. Harrington Family Collection.

Figure 31. James Ostler
buying fetishes from
Wilfred Cheama at
Pueblo of Zuni Arts and
Crafts.

terials used and animals represented, the intricacy of the carving, and unfamiliarity with the carver have made the job of buying Zuni fetishes much different from that of buying Zuni jewelry. When a store purchases a certain style of bolo or pendant, that trader knows that all subsequent purchases of that piece will be the same size, quality, and price. Cost of materials, size, number of inlay elements, and details of lapidary work are all parts of the equation for determining jewelry value. That is the way craftspeople as well as traders look at the market. With fetishes, the kind of stone (color and hardness), cost of stone, size of fetish, intricacy of carving, degree of polish, animal represented, and "beauty" of the carving all go into determining value. Generally speaking, for fetishes purchased for less than $10 there is little negotiation, and it is primarily size that determines the price. For pieces purchased for more than $10, the price is usually negotiated and all the factors enumerated above may come into play. In 1983 the highest price the tribal business paid for a fetish carving was $25; probably 75 percent fell in the range of the $3 to $10 category. In 1989 half the carvings were purchased for more than $12, and some were priced as high as $200. Clearly, what has spurred the increase in the number of carvers and the prices of their carvings has been the market demand for fetishes from Zuni.

In 1984 most fetishes were sold to stores that specialized in Indian goods, whereas in 1989 it is estimated that as many as one-third of the Zuni carvings were sold to stores which sold crystals, New Age materials, and supplies for self-healing. For these buyers, fetishes functioned in their more traditional Zuni religious role. The buyers wanted to know Zuni traditional beliefs about fetishes: what animals the fetishes represented, what powers particular animals might possess, what illnesses they might heal, and what strengths they might yield. Often these buyers would hold them in their hands or pass a crystal over them to determine whether to make the purchase.

One fetish buyer who wanted to become pregnant purchased a snake and an eagle fetish. Another woman purchased a mountain lion fetish to bury with her grandmother: cats were her favorite animal (Corilee Heinis, personal communication). Reportedly, a woman astronaut carried an eagle fetish into space (Leo Brereton, personal communication). At the end of the 1990 Russian-American summit conference Raisa Gorbachev was presented with a Zuni bear fetish as a farewell gift (Alice Killackey, personal communication, 1990). It has been suggested that fetishes are purchased as instruments for meditation with animal spirits or as totem animals, and that they may play some role in shamanism. After hearing these non-Zuni stories of fetish use, we might surmise that fetish carvings are bought because they have personality, they demonstrate their individuality with shape and color, they do not come off an assembly line, and they allow for, even call for, a personal, nonformalized search for knowledge about oneself and one's world.

In 1987 the tribal business received one

Figure 32. Turquoise mole. Faye Quandelacy. 1 1/2" long.

of its largest single orders for fetishes. The request came from the Houston Museum of Fine Arts for three hundred fetishes, all with bundles tied to them. They were to be used as gifts in the annual meeting of a Houston bank.

Alice Homer, daughter of Leekya and a very traditional artist, said in an interview that she did not make fetishes. She made carvings that could be taken to the appropriate priest by the buyer and made into fetishes. Thus it is how the stone is used that makes the difference between a carving and a fetish. Most carvers at Zuni would probably agree that they are making carvings and that whether or not those carvings are used as fetishes has to do with their owners, not the carver. Zuni carvers are also circumspect about what they carve and what they attach to the carving. One almost never sees feathers attached to a Zuni carving, as that is viewed as an encroachment on traditional beliefs. Zunis carve animals and only rarely any other forms. When a carver was asked if he ever carved kachinas in stone, he quickly said that he did not, as that would be improper. Many carvers place beads or arrowheads on the backs of their animals, called an "offering" (Fig. 32). In the past they were stone arrowheads found in the ruins, but now they are frequently carved simply and quickly of shell. The material used for wrapping is a beading thread that resembles the old sinew cords. Alice Homer was asked to attach a natural crystal to one of her carvings but refused because it was beyond her proper role as a carver.

Fetishes are still meaningful in Zuni tra-

Figure 33. Pipestone frog with turquoise inlay. Darren Shebola. 3" long.

ditional practices today. Although Zunis are more open about their beliefs than many of the other Pueblos of the Southwest, much esoteric knowledge is available only to men and women who have undergone initiation ceremonies. Therefore, this discussion of the use of fetish carvings is very general. Men still take fetishes hunting, and both men and women wear or carry them on their persons for protection from harm and to ensure success. Traditionally, it is more acceptable to barter for a fetish carving or other religiously meaningful object, but now many people simply buy them. They must be taken to a priest to be given the power to help the owner in hunting, and these ceremonies are done only by Zuni priests for other Zunis and only during the winter solstice. Fetishes can be used for protection as well as to cause evil or harm to others. In the past, hunting fetishes were held for the men of the village by the Antelope Society, but now each man keeps his own. Both men and women in medicine societies still use animal carvings for their healing rites. Some carvings made for these societies are a bit different from those made for hunting and for sale to outsiders, however, it was not proper for Zunis to say how they differ. Large carvings are also made for altars and shrines around the village. In the past, fetishes were placed in walls of homes and buried in fields for the fertility of crops. With the exception of special pieces for the medicine societies, carvers make the same style of pieces for both Zunis and non-Zunis. Generally, older people like the simpler, more stylized pieces, and younger ones prefer the

Figure 34. Chert wolf. Found in storeroom LA61955. Basketmaker III. c.650. A.D. Bureau of Indian Affairs. Excavated by Zuni Archaeological Project.

Figure 35. Andres Quam carving a jet bear on the wheel.

new, very realistic carvings. Finally, like non-Zunis, many people within the village purchase carvings as works of art, simply because they like the style or the materials.

Although both Zunis and non-Zunis use fetishes for religious purposes, the American public has become interested in the carvings as folk art. There has been a change in the tastes of American collectors in favor of small carved pieces, perhaps as a result of the increasing Japanese influence on American culture. Japanese society has a long tradition of admiring and collecting small precious carvings, *netsukes* and *ojimi-tame*, to ornament carrying boxes and small carvings set up within the home for aesthetic contemplation. Native American art as a whole has enjoyed a growth in international appreciation beginning in the early 1970s with the influential show and book *Two Hundred Years of American Indian Art* by Norman Feder and the Whitney Museum of American Art. This exhibition reintroduced Native American arts to the New York City art market, and both collecting and prices took off. Nontheless, fetish carving did not become popular until the 1980s, and Los Angeles and the media industry were the catalysts for subsequent interest in fetishes. Rather than collecting Indian art that would appreciate, buyers began to buy Indian art that had spiritual power. Actress Shelley Duval wore a fetish necklace in the film *Roxanne*, and Whoopi Goldberg collects the fetishes of Leonard Halate (Alice Killackey, personal communication, 1990). Today California is the largest market for fetish carvings.

It can be argued that it is the duality of appreciation of fetishes as objects of art and as objects of medicine which has fueled their popularity. Such interests are not mutually exclusive, and it is not unusual for the individual who started purchasing fetishes because of their medicinal qualities to buy them later as works of art. For both the trader in Zuni goods and the Zuni carver, it has presented some difficulty to make the switch from the buying and selling of crafts, which have a known and predictable price, to the buying and selling of Zuni art, whose price is neither known nor predictable. Fetishes in the traditional craft and usage category have maintained a fairly even growth curve in terms of price increases, generally not more than 20 percent in five years, but those fetishes that fall into the art category have increased in price as much as 500 percent in the same time period.

To the outsider, it may appear that the market determines what is made at the Pueblo. A board member of an Indian arts and crafts association headquartered in Santa Fe commented that Zunis are "manufacturers" and the craftspeople simply "jobbers". The element of truth in these labels is that handmade crafts are the major industry at Zuni, and like any craftspeople who depend on the sale of their work for their livelihood, Zunis find labor-saving techniques and sell more than one object at a time. Typically, a Zuni fetish carver brings in six to twelve carvings at once made out of the same rock and bearing a family resemblance (Fig. 36). Zunis have their own internally consistent stan-

Figure 36. Variety of animals cut from one large piece of serpentine. Max Laate.

dards—the set of beliefs that creates and reinforces all work that is done at Zuni. On the one hand, there is no such thing as an avant-garde artist at Zuni, and on the other hand, there is no such thing as a Zuni craftsperson who adheres to the dictates of an outside buyer. Everything at Zuni is done according to Zuni standards of beauty, craftsmanship, propriety, and ethics.

Figure 37. Antler eagle.
Herbert Hustito. 3" high.

The marvel of the Zuni social system is its ability to absorb outside influences without changing. Zunis have an elaborate and highly articulated religious system, as any of the writings of Cushing or Stevenson or even a visit to a contemporary ceremony clearly demonstrates. Zunis also have an extraordinary sense of propriety. If there is a dictum, it is that sloppiness is not tolerated. Innumerable examples in Zuni of the sense of propriety are seen in ordinary dress. Permed hair for both men and women, neatly pressed clothes, and carefully selected jewelry accents are everyday confirmations of this attitude.

Like everything else, artistry is not left to chance, and it is never left without comment. "Those Comanches moved too slowly and they weren't dressed right." "That group was unrehearsed." "I wish I could do work that well." "How does he paint so small?" "That silver work is not clean." "It looks good, but the stones are cracked and the solder is messy." "It is not polished well." "The bracelets are too plain." "The stones don't fit." "The painting of that kachina is not right: the horn is too long, and the colors are not right." What all of these overheard comments refer to are a community's standards that measure the quality of its art. No one is immune from criticism, no silversmith, no religious group, and no public official. It is difficult to imagine a community more critical of work produced or more exacting. Zunis sometimes say that they will not go to the kachina dances of particular kivas because the dances are too sloppy. Or conversely, they never miss the dances of particular kivas because they are so good. In a sense, at Zuni there is only public art, for everything is seen and everything discussed. Zuni is not a village of a thousand craftspeople because the outside market desires its jewelry; rather it is a village of a thousand craftspeople because its everyday life and traditional practices demand the perfection of its forms.

Zunis expect religious obligations to be met, and to fail is to risk sickness, injury, or even death. Such failure, therefore, can be seen either as personally foolhardy or threatening to others. To gain the respect of other Zunis, these duties must be performed well. One finds this same aesthetic in the Zuni appreciation of fetish carvings. Novelty may be mentioned, but what holds the Zunis' attention is the traditional piece that is executed well. It is as if the perfection of its form allows Zunis to see again the beauty of their tradition. It may be possible to isolate certain norms of Zuni arts and of fetish carving in particular which allow for this perfection of form.

To the outside observer who visits Zuni during a ceremonial period, what is most impressive is the seeming organization that directs so many people engaged in different tasks to a single outcome: batteries of ovens being fired and hundreds of loaves of bread being baked by teams of women all over the village, medicine

Figure 38. L to R: Louise Solomon, Lettie Caweyoka and Mita Waikenewa preparing mutton for Shalako ceremony.

Figure 39. Bread prepared for Shalako ceremony. Large quantities of food are prepared by families to feed the hundreds of people who participate in the winter ceremonial of Shalako.

Figure 40. Serpentine lizard.Lance Cheama. 7 1/2" long.

Figure 41. Shell fish. Terry Banteah. 3 3/4" long.

Figure 42. Serpentine fighting mountain lions. Wilfred Cheama. 7 1/4" long.

and kiva groups rehearsing songs, carcasses of beef and sheep being cut up and turned into stew. The casual observer may wonder how all this activity is coordinated. As one spends more time at Zuni, one begins to realize that no one at the top organizes the activity. Instead, everyone knows what to do because they have done it so many times before. In that sense it is not a new activity that needs to be organized but a collection of old ones that only needs to be given a starting time. Everyone, the young helper and especially the experienced hand, is vocal in his joking criticism of how things are supposed to be. This method of organization produces attention to detail based on the desire to perfect one's task. Each duty triggers the next, which must be executed with precise detail in order for the job to be done right.

When the tribal Arts and Crafts enterprise began doing trade shows in different cities, the staff members were reluctant to accept responsibilities for tasks that had not been done before, but it did not take them long to complete a checklist for the necessary equipment, supplies, and inventory. Once that was done, the preparation and execution of the shows proceeded like clockwork. Zunis may not like confronting unfamiliar complexity, but once a problem has been reduced to a series of details, their mastery is unmatched.

MASTERY OF DETAIL

Almost no facet of Zuni life escapes the devotion to detail. The Zuni jewelry industry concentrates on the articulation of lapidary detail.

Kiva groups and kachina dancers are criticized because they are not accurate in detail. Paintings are dismissed for their inattention to iconographic detail. The mastery of nuances reaches such importance that it sometimes becomes an end in itself. A Zuni potter, Randy Nahohai, has said that he wants to do a pot with a plumed serpent "as thick as my wrist" because then he can "put in all that detail." Zuni fetishes may come equipped with scales, or frogs with inlay spots, or eagles with disproportionately large outstretched wings so that the artist can articulate its feathers (Fig. 43). A logical extension of this Zuni preoccupation is miniaturization, for it is in the mastery of the tiny that the heroic proportions of detail are demonstrated (Fig 44). One finds this tendency in all the Zuni arts—in bracelets of inlay stones and shell that are smaller than a thumbtack, full paintings of religious scenes which are smaller than a postage stamp, and wildcats, frogs, or lizards that are carved in stone or bone and as small as a pea. Carvers often look over store cases of crafts and are quick to comment on how impressive they find the small pieces of jewelry or carving.

POLISH

As we have already seen, kiva groups are censured when they send out rain dancers whose dancing is rough and incomplete because it is not well rehearsed. The arts are also criticized for a lack of polish, and the literal shine of a piece may stand as a metaphor for completeness, finish, and grace. Polish is what one does at the stage of completion; it implies that everything else has been done. Jewelry is

Figure 43. Serpentine eagle. Daniel Quam. 3 1/4" wide.

Figure 44. Fluorite badger. Lance Cheama. 1 1/4" long.

Figure 45. Serpentine wolf. Fabian Homer. 2 1/2"long.

Figure 46. Serpentine colt. Vivella Bobelu. 2 1/4" long.

Figure 47. Jet mountain lion. Andres Quandelacy. 1 1/4" long.

Figure 48. Pipestone eagle head. Pernell Laate. 3 1/4" high.

made of brightly colored stones and shells that are set in silver and catch one's eye because of their shine. Fetishes are carved from materials that will reflect light: black jet, serpentine, ivory, malachite, and lapis. All Zuni jewelry and nearly all fetishes are buffed until they shine as an act of completion.

SOPHISTICATION

Another aspect of polish is the refinement of sophisticated behavior. Some outsiders may see Zuni as a relatively small village somewhat removed from the main trade routes, even though its archaeological history indicates that this isolation has not always existed. Many of the Pueblos, however, see Zuni as a place of sophistication. Certainly for the Navajos, Zuni is unequaled in the sophistication of its jewelry, ceremonial objects, and religious performances. Some Zunis in Gallup were surprised to hear a Santa Clara woman understand their conversation and speak to them in Zuni. On seeing their surprise, she said; "Yes, I can understand Zuni because my first husband was Zuni, but my second husband *dom dona bachu*" (is only a Navajo). The modern Zuni continues to present the image of being worldly wise. Grade-school children make the pilgrimage to Disneyland, and the high-school students are part of an ongoing exchange program with German families. Culturally and socially, Zunis are not shy and indirect individuals who hide their knowledge or experiences—rather they literally wear them on their sleeves. It is not at all unusual to see the well-dressed Zuni wearing a gift from a

Japanese friend, a German wristwatch, and a T-shirt from the Hard Rock Cafe. The point here is not that an individual is straying from a Zuni way of life, instead that he or she is knowledgeable about the people and places of the world.

Fetish carvers show their knowledge of the world by reading *National Geographic* and carving coelocanths, or using a chart of lizards of North America, or creating a stegosaurus with plates made of shell and encrusted with turquoise (Fig. 49). The sophistication of the carvers is also exemplified in how they talk about their materials and tools. They do not just use stone and bone, but Haitian or Baltic amber, silverado, Acoma or African jet, Sleeping Beauty turquoise, lapidolite, azurite, malachite, or Afghanistani lapis. Instead of just a grinder or drill they use a Fordham flexible shaft tool. Zunis are skilled specialists in all their endeavors—religious, social, or artistic—in contrast with the more general adaptation of nomadic people.

CRAFTSMANSHIP

In all Zuni things the ethic of good craftsmanship is evident. Zuni potter, Jack Kalestewa, prepares a kiln for firing his family's pottery by selecting manure of a certain size, then shaping each piece in squared blocks of uniform size, and finally laying the fuel as a mason would lay blocks for a house. His pots also show this care of fine craftsmanship, for they are thin-walled and extremely light, and his firings yield clean white pots with little trace of smoke. Good craftsmanship at Zuni means

Figure 49. Serpentine stegosaurus. Leonard Halate. 5 1/4" long.

Figure 50. Necklace with fetishes by various members of the Quandelacy family. Called a grandmother necklace because one like this was first made as a gift for Ellen Quandelacy, the head of the family.

Figure 51. Alabaster bears. Rickson Kalestewa. 3 3/4" high.

that the pieces fit, that the tolerances are very small, and that the work is clean. Invariably, the first comments made by a silversmith or carver when examining the work of others refer to the mastery of technique, the tightness of fit, the fineness of cutting, the heightened polish, the cleanness of the solder, and the strength of detail. Rarely does anyone comment on the design or its composition. It is as if design is taken for granted, is part of the community tradition, or is simply a result of good execution.

Another aspect of craftsmanship is individual style. "That's the way I carve," a fetish carver says. "Others may carve differently, but that's the way I carve." Artists become very upset if someone else copies their style. A carver recently came into the store to protest that his work was appearing in a mail-order catalog. "That's how my work gets copied," he complained. Within a family, styles are sometimes shared, and it is difficult to identify individual carvings except by a family name, such as with the Sheche family. Other families may share an approach to carving and can execute one another's work, but they do not trespass without permission. "She carves bears, I carve buffaloes, and he carves the mountain lions," one of the Quandelacy family said (Fig. 50). Because of these stylistic variations, it is possible to look at a display of several thousand Zuni fetish carvings and identify the individuals or families who made them.

Rarely does a craftsperson ask to be paid for his or her artistry or inventiveness or beauty of the work; instead, the potter, silversmith, or carver relates how hard the stone was, how difficult it was to dig the clay, how much wastage and fracture of the stones there was, or how long it took to make the piece. This ethic of craftsmanship may also be one of the reasons for the conservative nature of the Zuni arts sold by the traders. Because the Zunis were known to be marvelously skilled crafts-people, the trader's tactic has been to suggest work rather than to dictate (John Kennedy, personal communication, 1989).

Since fetish carvings are shaped by cutting away, one is now beginning to see more complex work: two bears coming out of one piece of rock, where the stone that is missing is more important than what remains (Fig. 51), and a pipestone lizard carved with a tail as thin as pencil lead (Fig. 29).

Despite the innovations that have occurred in fetish carving in the 1980s, fetishes still bear a close formal relationship to their antecedents of one hundred years ago. It is easy to confuse some modern carvings with those in the Smithsonian.

New materials and new tools are being used to carve fetishes, but the result is only that the carvers are allowed to come closer to perfecting the form. Carvers can be seen slicing multicolored stones so that the feet of the fox or the tips of his ears or the hump of a bear emerge from the stone in a different color. Engraving tools are used to detail feathers and fur and create ears of green serpentine that are turned so slightly that the animal appears poised in the instant before flight.

Figure 52.
Ellen Quandelacy at work.

Carvers are closely in tune with the market as conveyed to them by local dealers, and they respond to the need for certain animals. Most carvers sell their work within Zuni to a half dozen or so traders. A few also sell in Gallup, the nearest town. Only one or two families go farther afield to Santa Fe and Albuquerque. Individual middlemen sell on the road and take orders for large chain stores. Some of these middlemen are former school employees who found dealing in Zuni arts more lucrative than government employment. Most carvings are distributed through the business people at Zuni and Gallup who deal directly with the artists. Gallery owners come through on buying trips and personally select carvings to suit the tastes of their customers. Other contacts are made by sending representatives to the large California and Texas gift shows and to the Indian Arts and Crafts Association expositions held twice a year in a major western city. After the initial contacts are established many dealers order by mail or phone and have their selections shipped.

Carving, like all the arts at Zuni, is done in the home, thus allowing a great deal of flexibility for the individual. Most carvers have no other employment, or if they do, it is seasonal, such as road work or firefighting. Of course, when Zuni men are off in other parts of the West fighting fires, and there were many in the late 1980s, they are unable to carve. Frequently, a man's wife learns to carve in her husband's style and produces pieces while he is away. Generally, a carver does a few fetishes, often four to six of the same animal, and brings them in for sale as soon as they are finished. This process is repeated several times a week as the family needs cash. Even if he or she has a large order to fill, the animals are done a few at a time and presented to the buyer for payment.

MATERIALS

Most carvers purchase their raw materials from a trading post in Zuni. A few travel to Gallup or Albuquerque for reasons of price or selection. Some New Mexican owners of local alabaster and serpentine deposits come to Zuni with their materials and may trade rough stone for fetishes (Fig. 54). Most traders and Zunis prefer cash for their goods, but traders sometimes advance supplies in the hope of cornering the carver's output.

Many carvers still use local stones, but now most go to Arizona, where they request permission from the Apaches to collect serpentine along the Gila River. The Apaches say they have no use for the stone so the Zunis are welcome to gather it. Since prehistoric times the Zunis have had a wide trade network with raw materials coming in from the Pacific and Gulf coasts in the form of shells. The fact that older fetishes were made of the commonest of the softer local stones and then painted to obtain the correct directional color, however, indicates that the trade network was not adequate at that

Figure 53. Raw materials for sale at Turquoise Village.

time. Now the network is more sophisticated, with dealers going on long buying trips to the Orient in order to find novel and exotic stones and shell at low prices for the jewelry and carving market. The new, more expensive materials are used first by the more prominent artists, that is, those with more capital. If a stone is well received by the buying public, other artists will use it also. A distinctive material gives an artist an edge on the market for a while, and there is constant competition among the suppliers to provide new stones that will be in demand.

The most popular and least expensive of the stones used now are South Dakota pipestone or catlinite, jet, and serpentine in its various colors. Turquoise, although a staple for jewelry work, is used mostly for decorative touches on the carvings. Ivory is a recent and popular material, but because of the laws regulating the importation of elephant ivory, most of the material is now bought from the Inuit who mine fossilized walrus ivory from old middens. Because ivory is expensive, many artists buy animal bone from local butchers and bleach it to resemble the more valuable material. The use of bone and ivory is related to the more traditional use of deer and elk antler. Antlers are, of course, still very popular and are sold commercially for carvers' use. Artists who use this material complain of the terrible smell produced by the hot drill, and frequently their families insist that they work outside in a garage, carport, or shed. Malachite is another new material sometimes seen in jewelry and fetishes. It has a very noxious dust, which is reportedly poisonous, and

Figure 54. Ronnie Lunasee looking over serpentine brought in for sale by Joe Harris.

Figure 55. Dominican amber bear. Colvin Peina. 2 1/4" high.

great care is necessary to avoid breathing it. Lapis lazuli is another popular jewelry stone being used in carving. Like malachite, lapis is very hard and difficult to work without diamond drills. By and large, Zuni carvers prefer stones of medium hardness, which neither crumble during the operation nor are too hard for ordinary drill bits and wheels. Amber is a new material that has just the opposite problem of lapis and malachite, for it is very soft and if buffed too hard may lose its unique translucency.

Carvers have great ability to make maximum use of their materials. Figure 57 shows how an artist has cleverly used the central "column" of a large shell for a carving of a bird after the body of the shell had been used for necklace fetishes or jewelry inlays. Most carvers see an animal within a stone. Thus green serpentine naturally suggests lizards, turtles, frogs and snakes. The eagle head in Figure 58 came to mind when the artist noticed that the top layer of his block was white like the head of a bald eagle. Thus he capitalized on the natural property of the stone and, like all carvers, made an effort to bring out the beauty and unique qualities of his material.

TECHNIQUE

Raw materials purchased by the ounce or pound must be sawn into smaller pieces roughly the size and shape of the animal to be carved. Most carvers do not have power saws so there is some sharing of equipment for this process. The basic tool for carving is a motor to which are attached grinding wheels that can

Figure 56. Lance Cheama using a Fordham tool for details. The poster over his work bench shows the lizards of North America.

Figure 57. Bird made from central column of a large shell. Juana Homer.

Figure 58. Serpentine bald eagle head. Wilfred Cheama. 2 1/4" long.

also be used for cutting up larger stones. As mentioned before, Zuni carvers prefer medium-hard stones and generally do not use diamond wheels. A wheel called Brite Boy is used for smoothing, and then a buffing compound called <u>ZAM</u> is wiped on the carving and buffed with a rag or chamois wheel. Some carvers use emery paper rather than <u>ZAM</u> for the final polish, however. A dremel tool, a small hand-held power tool, is used for cutting details and inlays such as the heartline and eyes. After the animal is thought out or planned in the artist's head, the actual carving on the power wheel takes only five or ten minutes. Generally, a carver does half a dozen or so animals stage by stage to avoid changing the wheels—shaping, then polishing, and finally adding details. Sometimes another family member does the finishing. Those men and women who work in the new realistic style also use the more expensive Fordham tool for the details of scales and skins. In this case the animal may take a half hour to an hour to finish. The best equipment has a fan and a hose ventilating system. If a carver cannot afford this set-up, he or she works outside or near a door or window. Some families in which a number of people carve have a small studio with a row of power drills and ventilators (Fig. 60).

When asked about what makes a good Zuni carving, all the artists agreed that it is a high standard of craftsmanship: attention to detail, polish, and good finish. Some of the older carvers felt that the newer, more realistic style and untraditional animals were not truly

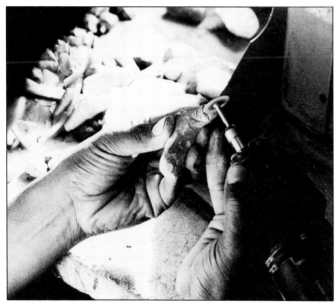

Figure 59. Herbert Hustito putting in fine details.

"Zuni" but that whatever brought income to another Zuni family was a good thing.

Carving, like all the arts at Zuni, is a family affair. Husbands teach wives, parents teach children, and the usual method of learning is to watch carefully the procedures of the teacher. No further class is necessary. Occasionally, a friend teaches another, but the student usually asks the teacher's permission to work in his or her style. One carver said that his in-laws taught him to carve so that he would be able to support his family: he quickly added that he would use only their techniques, not their style, which belonged to them. Even within a family, if one member develops a unique way of carving an animal, his brothers and sisters avoid doing that version. This respect for style is a matter of artistic pride, a feeling that each artist owns his or her own creations, and a concern for not encroaching on another Zuni's livelihood.

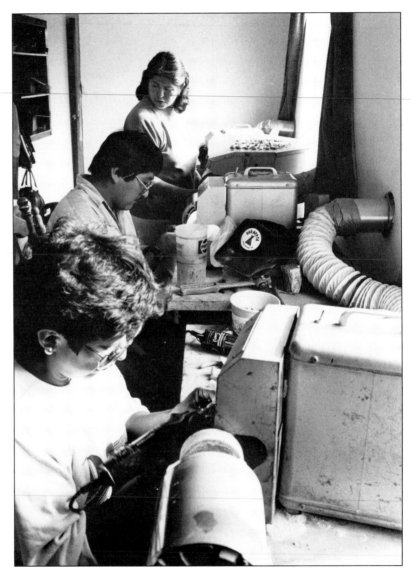

Figure 60. The Quandelacy family at work top to bottom: Albenita Yunie, Andres and Faye Quandelacy.

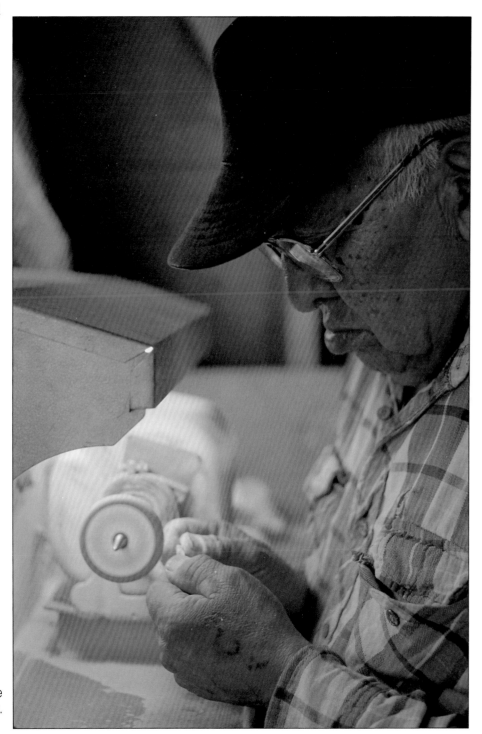

Figure 61. Leonard Halate at work.

THE LEEKYA FAMILY

The most famous carver of the earlier part of the twentieth century was Leekya Deyuse. Leekya is now the family's surname, because Leekya asked his children when they started school to use his first name as their last name, as there were too many other people named Deyuse then. Leekya's two daughters, Sarah and Alice, carried on his carving tradition. Alice spoke about her work shortly before her death in November 1988.

Other Leekya children—Elizabeth, Robert and Roger—are silversmiths. Alice's two children, Juana and Bernard Homer, Jr., carry on the family style. Alice learned in her twenties from her father, first by doing his sanding with emery cloth and then learning carving with an old-fashioned, hand-operated bow drill. Although Leekya used a hand grinder most of his life, at the end of his career he turned to electric equipment. Alice preferred to do stringing fetishes; occasionally, she made large table fetishes for a dealer in Gallup, but the stone was so heavy it became increasingly difficult for her to work on these pieces.

Most of the family work consists of bear fetishes. Many hunters came to Alice for bears which they then took to a priest for a ceremony before the hunt. The family still uses a lot of local stone and goes to Corn Mountain (Dowa Yalanne) to gather raw materials.

Sarah Leekya learned carving by helping her father with his polishing when she was twelve or thirteen. She began to carve on her own about two years after her father's death in

Figure 62. Serpentine mole. Sarah Leekya. 2 1/4" long.

Figure 63. Jet skunk. Leekya Deyuse, 1931. 1 1/4" long. Heard Museum. 1707-455.

Figure 64. Alabaster bear. Bernard Homer. 3 " long.

1966. Dealers urged her to continue in her father's style and gave her a book with pictures of his work. Sarah is both a carver and a jeweler, depending on the demand. The animals Sarah is noted for are coyotes, wolves, and bears in serpentine, alabaster, and green snail shell that she buys in Gallup. Her carvings have the same delicately carved pointed ears that Leekya's did.

So famous was their father that the children have carried on his style to please dealers and collectors. One dealer insists that the family put a small silver tag marked <u>Leekya</u> on its bear necklaces. The family style is one of rounded, pleasing forms with shallow cuts or grooves rather than sharp lines and contours.

Figure 65.
Pipestone bear.
Juana Homer.
3" long.

THE SHECHE FAMILY

Thelma Sheche learned carving from her father, Theodore Kucate, who died in the early 1980s in his late nineties. She helped her father by polishing his carvings, but she herself did not start carving until about 1972. She used to be a silversmith but has given her tools to her children and does carving full time. Thelma's husband, Aaron, has been carving for twenty years. She is very proud of the fact that her two teenage granddaughters, Marnela and Trisha Kucate, started carving so young and are already quite good at it. Each family member works on his or her own pieces: Thelma, her children, Arden and his wife Carmelia, and Lorendina, as well as her grandchildren. The family members carve the symbol ATS into each piece.

Theodore Kucate used to make fetishes from rocks he found along the river (Fig. 30). He carved sheep for the Navajos to use in protecting their flocks and traded his work to the Santo Domingo and Oklahoma Indians. It is more appropriate to trade for fetishes that are going to be used for religious purposes than to give money for them. The Kucates traveled and performed traditional Zuni dances (Fig. 68). Theodore was also a tribal councilman. In the 1920s a visiting government official from Washington, D.C., gave him a copy of Frank Hamilton Cushing's *Zuni Fetiches* and he began making replicas of the pieces illustrated there. Since the publication first came out in 1883, the color illustrations were done by chromolithography rather than photography. Thus some sub-

Figure 66. L to R: Lorandina, Thelma and Aaron Sheche.

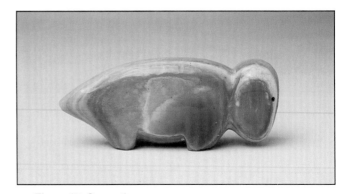

Figure 67. Serpentine lynx. Aaron Sheche. 3 3/4" long. Based on Smithsonian fetish shown in Figure 21.

tleties in the colors and materials of the originals are lost. The family continues to reproduce the "Cushing" fetishes, usually in the four-to-six-inch size, although Thelma said they sometimes do one "as large as a shoebox" and stringing size fetishes as well. The family keeps a set of cardboard templates at the workbench as a reminder of the prices they get for the various sizes.

The Sheches collect materials along the Salt River in Arizona and use other traditional materials like alabaster, jet, and travertine. They do only traditional Zuni animals, that is, the hunters of the six directions.

Figure 68. Old newspaper photograph of Theodore Kucate and Thelma Sheche.

Figure 69. Serpentine bird. Lorandina Sheche. 2 3/4" long.

Figure 70. Alabaster male and female coyotes. Aaron Sheche. 4 1/4" long. Based on Smithsonian fetish shown in Figure 10.

Figure 71. Alabaster mole. Aaron Sheche. 2 1/2" long.

RHODA QUAM

Rhoda learned to carve in 1971 from her mother, Annie Gasper. Her mother does not carve anymore but makes jewelry. Rhoda works on jewelry with her husband, Raybert Kantena —he does the silver work and she sets the stones. She is trying to teach her two sons and one daughter in the summers when they are home from school. Rhoda started with shell, but amber and ivory are her favorite materials. Her typical animals are the howling coyote, deer, and bears, and she uses a nature book to study different poses. She also makes stringing fetishes and standing fetishes up to five inches and finds carving faster than making silver. She and her husband help one another with their work. Their specialty is setting sun faces into ivory and antler. Rhoda believes a good fetish takes more time than a mediocre one and has a lot of details.

Figure 72.
Rhoda Quam

Figure 73. Alabaster deer with inlaid turquoise heartline. Rhoda Quam. 3 1/4" high.

Figure 74. Scotty dog.
Annette Tsikewa.
1 1/2" long.

Figure75. Serpentine
cat.. Annette Tsikewa.
2 1/4" long

Figure 76. Dolomite ram.
Annette Tsikewa.
2 1/2" long.

Figure 77. Bear.
Bill Tsikewa.
2 3/4" long.

Figure 78.
Lapis frog.
Annette Tsikewa.
3/4" long.

ANNETTE TSIKEWA AND EDDINGTON HANNAWEEKE

Eddington's family makes jewelry, but Annette comes from one of the great Zuni carving families. Her father was David Tsikewa, and her grandfather was Teddy Weahkee. Annette learned by helping her parents with their buffing. Now she and her husband work together: Eddington draws the animals on paper for Annette to carve and then she does the rough carving and shaping and he the detail work and buffing. She started with shell but prefers ivory, amber, and malachite. They use a diamond drill for the harder materials. They are proud of the fact that they do twenty-five different animals, including fish, coyotes, bears, pigs, woodpeckers and tadpoles, and both feel that the styles today are better and more varied than ever before. Like most carvers they regard finish, shine, and precise detail as the characteristics of a fine fetish. They do stringing fetishes and some up to six inches tall. Once they were given a piece of branch coral and turned it into a tree with birds and animals carved to appear as though they were perched on the branches. They never fail to examine their work carefully to be sure it is perfect, and they will not reglue a piece if it breaks. Annette remembers her grandfather was famous for his dolls with tablitas (Fig. 24 and 28). Her four-year-old is already picking up pieces of shell around the workbench and trying to make things out of them.

LEONARD HALATE

Leonard, born in 1914, has been carving since he was a young man. While herding sheep, he picked up white stone and carved bears, wolves, coyotes, and water animals, as well as animals he saw in the fields. His uncle, Ha ta pupu, taught him the necessary skills. Later Leonard learned silversmithing and made mostly rings and earrings, but he has given it up in favor of carving. His style has not changed from the time he first learned, in the 1940s, although today he buys stones rather than finding them. His favorites are spotted serpentine, bright red pipestone, and large solid antlers, but it is the texture and color of the materials that attract him. He makes stringing fetishes and large serpentine pieces and got the idea for his "alligators" from pieces in the Pueblo of Zuni Arts and Crafts store. Leonard likes his buffaloes best and uses bird claws for the horns. Preferring large animals, he even makes dinosaurs, whose pictures he has seen in books. He thinks his work is still good, although he says the young men use more detail in their carving.

Figure 79.
Leonard Halate

Figure 80.
Serpentine dinosaur
Leonard Halate.
5 1/2" long.

Figure 81.
Antler alligator with fish in its mouth.Leonard Halate.
8 3/4" long

Figure 82.
Herbert Halate

HERBERT HALATE

Herbert, about thirty, learned when he was eleven or twelve by watching his father, Leonard Halate. Starting with shell, he soon learned to use stone, especially alabaster, serpentine, and pipestone. Herbert prefers the various types of serpentine, and he likes jet but it frequently cracks when polished. His repertoire includes all animals but his favorites are rams and buffaloes. The sides of his animals are often decorated with designs from petroglyphs seen around Zuni. Four of his sisters—Reva, Vella, Marvelita, and Pansy also carve. Herbert works on and off at fetish carving of all sizes up to eight by eight inches and smoothness of surface is the quality he seeks.

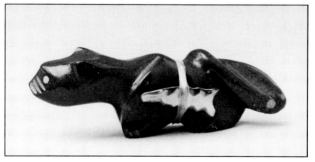

Figure 83.
Pipestone mountain lion.
Herbert Halate.
3 1/4" long.

GARY ACQUE

Gary learned from Herbert Halate in 1988, when construction work was slow, and used Herbert's tools at first. He makes bears, owls, and badgers and has tried elephants and mountain lions with petroglyphs on their sides. He asked Herbert's permission to use his style. First he chose pipestone, as it is soft and easy to work, and later he went on to serpentine and alabaster. Some stones he buys by the pound and others he collects along the Salt River in Arizona. He made jewelry in the 1970s and retains his tools should the need arise to return to silver working.

Gary's grandfather, Old Man Acque, was a famous carver. Gary has done repairs on his grandfather's work and has one of his grandfather's fetishes, which he uses in hunting. Now he is teaching his thirteen-year-old son, Garrick, how to carve. He makes his own arrowpoints for attachment, some of them in turquoise. He has not made stringing fetishes yet, but has done a few large pieces on special order. Although he sells mainly in Zuni, he also wholesales in Albuquerque and may rent a table at the Santa Fe Indian Market. Working alone, he can make twenty to twenty-five pieces in one day, doing his own rough sawing, carving, and finishing. He uses his imagination to interpret the animals and produces a distinctive fetish with an eye-catching style. Gary buys antlers in the store, because they are soft and easy to work, but they do not take details well and tend to flake off during carving. He picks rocks carefully to get ones with no cracks. It took him six weeks to perfect his carving, and his style changes according to what sells.

Figure 84.
Pipestone ram.
Gary Acque. 2 1/4" high.

Figure 85.
Necklace with birds and
bears. Verna Noche.

VERNA NOCHE

Verna is the daughter of famous carvers Sam and Lita Delena. Verna says she learned from her mother, who in turn learned from her father George Cheechee. When Verna graduated from high school, she worked at Maalco and later Turquoise Village so she does not have much time to carve, except in the evenings. Her husband is a firefighter and helps her buff the fetishes in the winter when he is not employed. After starting with shell, she now works mostly in turquoise, coral and serpentine, but has not tried lapis or malachite. Verna does only stringing fetishes, birds and bears, although her husband is experimenting with larger pieces. She gets her materials mostly at Turquoise Village, where she also sells her finished products. She wants to start doing larger pieces, but finding time is a problem.

60

THE QUANDELACY FAMILY

Ellen is the head of the Quandelacy family and learned from her father, Johnny Quam. The other carvers in the family are Albenita, Georgiann, Faye, Barlow, Stewart and Andres. Ellen's first carvings were antler prairie dogs and owls, and she started her children and grandchildren with the same animals. Ivory and amber are the most expensive materials, so she likes to come to the flea market in Albuquerque to buy old amber beads from the African traders. Her family is noted for work in jet, but there is no longer high-quality jet found locally. She prefers jet from Africa, as it is the hardest, whereas the jet from Pennsylvania is soft and cracks easily, an important consideration since it has to be cut with the grain. The family gathers stones on the Salt River Apache Reservation. They also obtain local Zuni sandstone, dolomite from Mexico, and alabaster from a tombstone company near Nambe. The Quandelacys buy red shell from a man who dives for it in the Gulf of Mexico. Clam shell is sliced in strips and then carved.

The family is well known for its stringing fetishes and sometimes combines its pieces with heishe sold door to door by a man from Santo Domingo. The Quandelacys polish the fetishes first and then drill them, a technique they believe keeps the carvings from breaking. Ellen does demonstrations in other parts of the country and brings work along to sell. She also sells to tour group members who are brought to her house. When asked if it was proper for a Zuni woman to wear a fetish necklace, she said

Figure 86. Quandelacy family from left to right: Andres, Georgiann, Albenita Yunie, Faye, Brian Yunie

Figure 87. Fossilized ivory Corn Maiden. Faye Quandelacy. 2 1/2" high.

yes, but that they could not keep them long enough to wear. Albenita said a woman in Gallup had bought one of hers off of her neck.

Each Quandelacy has his or her own style in addition to the bear with a high arched back and heartline for which the family is noted. Andres is famous for his standing bears and a sinuous mountain lion with its tail curled across its back. Barlow originated the bear with a fish in its mouth, and Ellen is noted for her horses. Albenita Quandelacy Yunie has been helping her husband learn to carve, and together they have been making howling coyotes. Faye attended the Institute of American Indian Arts and prefers to make larger sculpture. Since she cannot afford large pieces of alabaster, she buys scrap from sculptor Doug Hyde. She has shown at the Fenn Gallery in Santa Fe and is known for her women and children and corn maidens along with a fatter version of her brother's mountain lion. The Quandelacys go to the Santa Fe Indian Market and take orders, and although customers commonly commission unusual animals like cats and monkeys, the family prefers to do traditional Zuni animals. Ellen thinks a good fetish for hunting must have an arrowhead on its back in addition to displaying well-engraved lines and a high finish.

Figure 88. Dolomite bear. Stewart Quandelacy. 2 1/2" long.

Figure 89. Jet fox. Georgiann Quandelacy. 1 1/2" long.

Figure 90. Jet bear with fish. Faye Quandelacy 1 1/2" long.

Figure 91. Serpentine bear. Barlow Quandelacy. 2 1/4" long.

RONNIE LUNASEE AND
FABIAN TSETHLIKAI

Ronnie, who started to carve at age sixteen, was taught by his brother-in-law, Melvin Sandoval, but it took two years for him to mature. He likes dolomite and serpentine, which he buys at Gallup, and sells his work in Zuni and occasionally in Albuquerque. He carves frogs and bears, especially the sitting variety, the largest of which is four inches high. He regards a creative mind as the most important part of fetish carving and often dreams about the animals he will carve. A serpentine lizard was selected for the museum exhibit because it would take a polish like glass, a quality he values. Although he learned from Melvin Sandoval, Ronnie does the more traditional stylized fetishes, leaving Melvin to do the new realistic type.

Ronnie taught his cousin Fabian Tsethlikai, and the two young men work together on opposite ends of the wheel.

Figure 92. Ronnie Lunasee (left) and Fabian Tsethlikai (right) in their workshop in the family garage.

Figure 93. Serpentine fish. Ronnie Lunasee. 3" long

Figure 94. Serpentine horned toad. Ronnie Lunasee. 3" long.

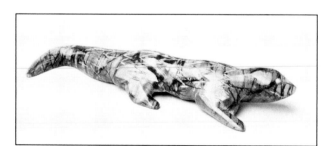

Figure 95. Picasso marble lizard. Melvin Sandoval I 4 3/4" long.

MELVIN SANDOVAL

Melvin has been carving for several years. He generally does only four animals: lizards, horned toads, coyotes, and moles. He has also carved large sculptures—in particular, a buffalo in marble and serpentine. From San Felipe Pueblo, Melvin attended school in Bernalillo and married a Zuni woman. He has no formal art training but learned on his own by looking at books and working at first only with hand tools. He hammered out the pieces of stone and put in details with a knife. Now he owns motor tools, including a Fordham and a dremel, and his favorite materials are marble and Picasso marble.

Figure 96.
Melvin Sandoval

Figure 97. Serpentine
badger. Melvin Sandoval.
3 1/2" long.

COLVIN AND CLAUDIA PEINA

Colvin has been carving since about 1985 and learned from his uncles Raymond Haloo and Miguel Haloo, who no longer carves. He has developed a highly personal style based in part on illustrations in *National Geographic* and his own imagination. One of his pieces won first prize in the Gallup Ceremonial in 1988 and this encouraged him to enter a piece this year. He used to make jewelry, but when business was down he took up carving and finds he likes it better. Colvin's favorite materials are ivory, antler, and bone, but he also works in serpentine, amber, and treated turquoise. He sells in Zuni exclusively.

Colvin's favorite forms are lizards, bears, turtles, and corn maidens. The maidens have in the background a small cliff village that Colvin says is meant to be Mesa Verde. Attention to detail is most important in order to depict the true appearance of an animal. He has now taught his sister, Claudia Peina, to make bears.

Figure 98. Colvin and Claudia Peina

Figure 99. Serpentine bear with turquoise necklace. Colvin Peina. 2 1/2" high.

Figure 100. Ironwood Corn Maidens. Colvin Peina. 5 3/4" high.

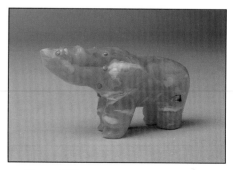

Figure 101. Baltic amber bear. Colvin Peina.

Figure 102. Antler bear. Ramie Haloo. 3" high.

ANDRES AND JEWELITA QUAM

Andres's mother, Rosalia, taught him the craft in 1978, and she and her husband, Emerson Anderson Quam, were prominent carvers in the 1960s and 1970s. Jewelita, Andres's wife, does stringing and table fetishes as well. Andres stopped carving stringing fetishes but still makes flat eagle pendants out of shell. He now concentrates on the standing bears with their heads turned sharply over their shoulders as if startled, a form that he adapted from his uncles Ramie and Miguel Haloo.

Figure 103. Jewelita, Cynthia Quam and Andres Quam.

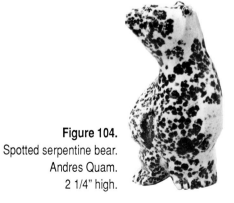

Figure 104. Spotted serpentine bear. Andres Quam. 2 1/4" high.

WILFORD AND FAYLENA CACHINI

Faylena used to be a jeweler but has been carving since 1986, when she learned from her former husband, Eldred Quam, another son of Emerson and Rosalia Quam. When she moved home, she taught her brother, Wilford. She does howling coyotes, bears, turtles, and mountain lions, and he does frogs. Her ideas come from the rocks themselves, and her preferred mediums are alabaster and serpentine. Since they own only one motor, the brother and sister take turns and work near the front door to keep the dust out of the house.

Figure 105. Wilford and Faylena Cachini with Emerson Quam.

Figure 106. Spotted serpentine fox. Faylena Cachini. 1 3/4" long.

Figure 107. Serpentine badger. Wilford Cachini. 2 1/2" long.

Figure 108. Tyler Quam.

TYLER QUAM

Tyler, aged twenty, is a son of Emerson and Rosalia Quam and, like his parents, works in the traditional style. He learned from his parents and started using their equipment in 1984. He likes to carve buffaloes, horses, frogs, and turtles in green serpentine and turquoise. He worked in tigereye once but had to use a diamond drill, which is more expensive.

Figure 109. Horse. Tyler Quam. 2 1/2" long.

Figure 110. Turquoise frog earrings. Andrew and Laura Quam. Each 3/4" long.

Figure 111. Eldred Quam.

Figure 112. Spotted serpentine frog Georgette Quam. 2" long

Figure 113. Bear. Eldred Quam 2" high.

ULYSSES MAHKEE

Ulysses learned carving in about 1985 by watching his brother-in-law, Andres Quam. His wife, Colleen, helps by polishing. Ulysses originated the flat-sided ram with petroglyphs. He likes serpentine, most medium-hard stones and dolomite, which is relatively expensive at four dollars per pound. He works a little with ivory, especially for buffaloes, which, along with eagles and lizards, are his favorite animals. He works in a small bedroom with a bed and crib nearby. Ulysses is one of the few carvers who does not believe in putting arrowheads on the backs of his animals.

Figure 114.
Dolomite buffalo.
2 3/4" long.

Figure 115.
Ulysses Mahkee in
bedroom studio.

Figure 116. Dolomite ram
with petroglyphs.
2 3/4" long.

EMERY AND DAISY ERIACHO

Emery left Zuni and lived in southern California for many years. When he returned, he learned carving from his wife, Daisy, who does stringing fetishes. Daisy in turn learned carving from her previous husband, Andres Quam. Emery gets stones in the rough and cuts them first on his trim saw and then cuts them into little rectangles for bears. Emery has been using Death Valley serpentine, which looks like onyx, and his "rockhound" friends in California and elsewhere supply him with new and unusual materials. In exchange, he sends them his fetishes. So far, Emery has been doing bears, but he is trying to make other animals. To save money on materials he uses steak bones bought from butchers for stringing fetishes. One round bone makes three small bears, each with a graceful curve. Emery has a strong feeling for the various stones and their properties.

Figure 117. Emery and Daisy Eriacho with Andrea Quam.

Figure 118. Jet turtle. Andrew Quam. 1 1/4" long.

Figure 119. Picasso marble bear. Emery Eriacho. 2 1/4" long.

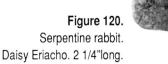

Figure 120. Serpentine rabbit. Daisy Eriacho. 2 1/4"long.

70

DAN PONCHO

Dan is an army veteran, and when he returned to Zuni he learned to carve from his in-laws (the Quams). He and his son Alex work in a small workshop in their backyard doing simple, traditional carvings of frogs and snakes. Alex specializes in snakes and has an order for five hundred of them for a dealer in Ramah.

Figure 121. Alex Poncho (left) and Dan Poncho (right).

Figure 122. Serpentine wolf. Dan Poncho. 2" long.

Figure 123. Serpentine bear. Dan Poncho. 2 1/2" long.

Figure 124. Serpentine coyote or fox. Dan Poncho.2 1/2" long.

Figure 125.
Clive Hustito.

CLIVE HUSTITO

Clive (no relation to Herbert Hustito) learned on his own after gaining considerable experience carving miniature kachinas and painting in oils and tempera. He has been carving for two years and prefers to work in shell and serpentine. Clive has made frogs, badgers, lizards, deer, horses, bears, and even an aardvark he saw in his nephew's biology book.

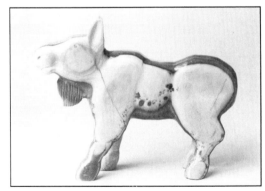

Figure 127. Serpentine cow moose. 6" long.

Figure 126. Serpentine bull moose. 2" long.

THE CHEAMA FAMILY

Perhaps the biggest change in Zuni fetish carving in the last few years is the development of the highly realistic style. The carvers of this style, mostly young men in their late teens and early twenties, were encouraged by Don Sharp, an administrator with the federal Young American Conservation Corps.

Although the approach was new, they learned in the traditional way through their family connections, but Sharp encouraged their work and found new markets for them.

The leaders of this new style and the first to use it are the Cheama brothers: Daniel Quam, Lance, Fabian, and Wilfred. Daniel is the eldest and is much respected by his brothers as the best carver in the family. He started carving in 1982 and before that made jewelry. He believes he was the first to do realistic carvings. Lance learned in 1986 from his older brother Daniel. His favorite animals are lizards, snakes, badgers, and weasels, all of which have become the trademarks of the Cheama family. He sold a bear to a hunter and a frog for a rain dancer to use as a weight on his headdress. The family's preferred materials are ivory and serpentine. Joe Harris of Silver City, comes to Zuni with good serpentine (without fractures), a material that suits the animals the Cheamas carve best. Sometimes they carve in lapis, amber, and turquoise. The brothers keep animal books and use them for details of species that do not live in the area and to ensure that their carvings have both delicacy and life.

Figure 128. L to R: Lance Cheama, Daniel Quam, Wilfred Cheama, and Fabian Cheama.

Figure 129. Jet fly. Wilfred Cheama.

Figure 130. Serpentine rattlesnake with turquoise rattles and coral tongue. Wilfred Cheama. 2 1/2" diameter.

Figure 131. Serpentine fox. Fabian Cheama. 2 1/2" long.

It takes Lance about an hour and a half to make a piece, and his wife, Karen Zuni, does the sanding. He uses a Fordham tool with different tips for details. He is beginning to win prizes for his work: the Museum of Northern Arizona awarded him three honorable mentions and a second prize since he began carving. Lance was a firefighter in 1988, but in 1989 he broke his leg and while recuperating had more time to devote to carving. Although he was offered a job carving in the workshop of a dealer in Gallup, he prefers to work at home. He would like to do African animals—his brother Wilfred makes lions and once made a giraffe. Lance loves to carve lizards and has a poster of the lizards of North America over his workbench. The brothers' styles are so close as to be almost indistinguishable, and all the Cheamas feel that patience and slow, careful work make a good carving. People want quality, the brothers say.

Figure 132. Serpentine buffalo. Daniel Quam. 2 1/4" long.

Figure 133. Serpentine bobcats. Wilfred Cheama.

Figure 134. Serpentine badger. Lance Cheama. 2" long.

Figure 135. Karen Zunie, Lance Cheama and Ashley Cheama.

HERBERT HUSTITO

Herbert, twenty-seven, learned at age eighteen from Daniel Quam. In 1989 he won best in show in the Museum of Northern Arizona, Flagstaff for an eagle of antler and he earned a second prize there in 1988. Herbert is proud of the fact that he is growing in ability and in public recognition. His favorite material is antler, and he also works with turquoise, serpentine, and fossilized ivory which in hardness are about the same as antler. He has not made stringing fetishes yet, although he did a miniature carving from the tip of an antler. In the past he has made eagles, badgers, bears, cobras, a beaver on a dam, a buffalo with her calves, and even camels for the Palestinian traders who set up at Zuni during the jewelry boom of the 1970s. He works from pictures in some cases, such as for carvings of a rattlesnake eating a frog and a boa squeezing a rabbit.

Herbert uses twenty-two different tools for details as well as a simple grinding stone. Diamond drills are employed for the eyeholes, an operation sometimes done by his wife, Alfina, who does the buffing for him as well. He is teaching her to carve, and she was able to continue while he was out firefighting. Herbert maintains that a good fetish carver must love both his work and animals (he had six dogs as a boy) but must also use imagination.

Figure 136. Herbert Hustito and his son.

Figure 137. Serpentine ram. Herbert Hustito. 1 3/4" long.

Figure 138.
Kent Banteah

Figure 139.
Terry Banteah

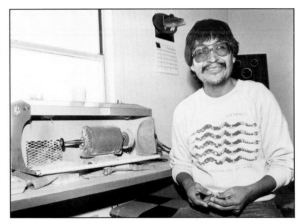

Figure 140.
Serpentine
rattlesnake.
Kent Banteah.
3" long.

KENT AND TERRY BANTEAH

Although Kent has been carving only since 1988 his work displays the precision of the new realistic style with carefully rendered details of fur and claws. He learned by watching his friend Fabian Cheama, one of the Cheama brothers, who are the leading artists in this style. Soon Kent bought his own tools and since being laid off is now back to carving. He started out doing simple frogs, but now he does snakes, fish, whales, beavers, elephants, and walruses. Kent gets his ideas from books and magazines such as *National Geographic* and *Field and Stream*. He prefers to carve southwestern reptiles in ivory and turquoise. Although he started off with alabaster, he also likes serpentine and shell, especially abalone. Most of his materials are purchased in Gallup but he goes to Socorro for the best serpentine. A good carving in his opinion is one with a lot of detail and imagination, and he prefers to work on pieces primarily in the range of three to five inches. He does inlay work on turtles with turquoise and although he has never done jewelry, his wife is a jeweler. He taught fetish carving to his brother Terry and has made bears for his cousin's religious society. Although the two brothers now work together in the house, Kent is building a new workshop. They have a Natural Light beer fish poster over their workbench which supplies models for pike, perch, trout and bass. Like the other realistic carvers, they use a Fordham tool for the fine detailed work.

PERNELL AND MAX LAATE

Pernell has been carving since 1988. No one taught him, but since he had made kachinas he did have artistic experience. He works only when he feels like it and is inspired to make something. Pernell taught his brother Max, who also paints on canvas, and the two usually make one or two pieces a day. At first they carved only in pipestone and serpentine because they were less familiar with other materials. Now they like to use bone, antler, and cow horn and perhaps will try to work with horse hooves. They also want to use fossilized seashell because it polishes to a glass-like surface. Perhaps because of their background in kachina carving, they feel that it is not proper to attach points and beads to their carvings.

The brothers like to carve fish and have done small eels, birds, and cats and hope to produce larger animals soon. Although they use *Outdoor Life* and *Fish and Stream* as sources, the prefer to interpret animals in their own way. They have a sheep ranch at Nutria, New Mexico and like the out-of-doors, taking frequent hikes up Dowa Yalanne, which towers over their home. Although he has not been working long Pernell won a third prize in the Museum of Northern Arizona show in 1989. Each piece the brothers carve is different, and although they may represent the same animals, a different characteristic is brought out each time. Pernell wants to do African animals, and both young men believe their future pieces will have a more detailed and lifelike appearance.

Figure 141. Pernell Laate (left) and Max Laate (right).

Figure 142. Pipestone big mouth bass. Pernell Laate. 4 1/2" long.

Figure 143. Pipestone fish. Max Laate. 8 1/2" long.

Figure 144. Pipestone ducks. Pernell Laate. 1 1/2 long.

Figure 145. Pipestone butterfly. 3" high.

Figure 146.
Rickson Kalestewa

Figure 147. Alabaster mountain lion. 4 1/4" long.

RICKSON KALESTEWA

Rickson learned carving by watching his brother-in-law, Darrell Westika. He tried silver jewelry first, which he studied in high school, but when silver got expensive in the 1970s, he went into carving. Rickson makes traditional fetishes with black jet and inlay as well as his more distinctive style in which the animals' heads rise directly from their backs. He prefers alabaster in different colors, because it is a stone of medium hardness and thus is easiest to carve. He does animals of all sizes, both standing and sitting, and although he wants to make necklace fetishes he does not have the proper drill bits. In 1989 he began making a workshop out of an old building next to his house. When it is finished he will buy new equipment, enabling him to work on harder rock. The arrowheads he makes himself out of shell.

Rickson carves mostly bears and mountain lions, the latter being the more difficult to do. He wants to make his work more interesting, and now that he has been laid off from his job at the telephone company he can spend more time on fetish carving. He feels that a good fetish is of clean, attractive stone with a high polish and that artists should put extra time into their carving. When he and a friend were in the mountains, he saw a mountain lion on a rock outcropping and it hissed to scare him away. His friend later saw the lion around their village, so he now makes the carvings with a new respect. He won second prize at the 1988 Museum of Northern Arizona show. His materials come from Gallup because the prices and variety are better there, and he sometimes trades his fetishes for stone. His parents, Jack and Quanita Kalestewa, are famous potters who take his work to Santa Fe to sell.

Figure 148. Malachite bear by Jimmy Yawakia. 1 3/4" long.

The carving of small animals for use as protective charms goes back at least 1500 years in the Zuni area. The descendants of the ancient inhabitants continue to use them to protect themselves, their crops, flocks, and houses. In the twentieth century an additional use, that of art object made to sell to outsiders, has been added to fetishes' traditional purposes.

Zuni artists make the fetishes of today with the same care and in the same forms as those that are used within the village. The Zuni world has widened and unusual materials from as far away as China, southeast Asia and Afghanistan are used in modern carving. Art is very much a family concern as can be seen from the interviews with contemporary carvers. More men and women are teaching their spouses, probably because there is an expanding market for fetishes. When a divorce occurs, each spouse teaches his or her new partner. The children of Emerson and Rosalia Quam, with all their spouses, make up the largest family carving style in Zuni. Additionally, many young men, usually under the age of thirty, are learning carving from their close friends, a new trend in this ever expanding art form. Undoubtedly many more changes lie ahead as fetishes become more and more appreciated outside of Zuni and the Southwest.

FAMILY CHARTS

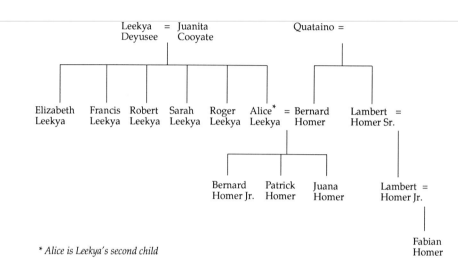

We found the genealogy research to be more
difficult than we anticipated. The family lines
may not be as clear as these charts suggest.

Leekya = Juanita
Deyusee   Cooyate

Quataino =

Elizabeth   Francis   Robert   Sarah   Roger   Alice* = Bernard   Lambert =
Leekya   Leekya   Leekya   Leekya   Leekya   Leekya   Homer   Homer Sr.

Bernard   Patrick   Juana   Lambert =
Homer Jr. Homer   Homer   Homer Jr.

Fabian
Homer

Alice is Leekya's second child

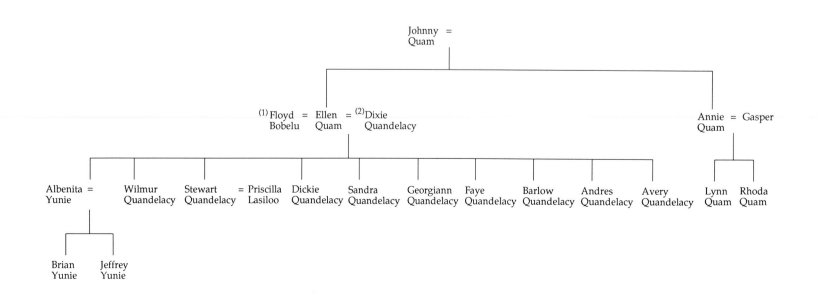

Johnny =
Quam

(1)Floyd = Ellen = (2)Dixie
Bobelu   Quam   Quandelacy

Annie = Gasper
Quam

Albenita =   Wilmur   Stewart   = Priscilla   Dickie   Sandra   Georgiann   Faye   Barlow   Andres   Avery   Lynn   Rhoda
Yunie   Quandelacy   Quandelacy   Lasiloo   Quandelacy   Quandelacy   Quandelacy   Quandelacy   Quandelacy   Quandelacy   Quandelacy   Quam   Quam

Brian   Jeffrey
Yunie   Yunie

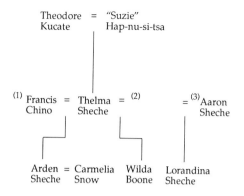

Theodore = "Suzie"
Kucate   Hap-nu-si-tsa

(1) Francis = Thelma = (2)   = (3) Aaron
    Chino   Sheche   Sheche

Arden = Carmelia   Wilda   Lorandina
Sheche Snow   Boone   Sheche

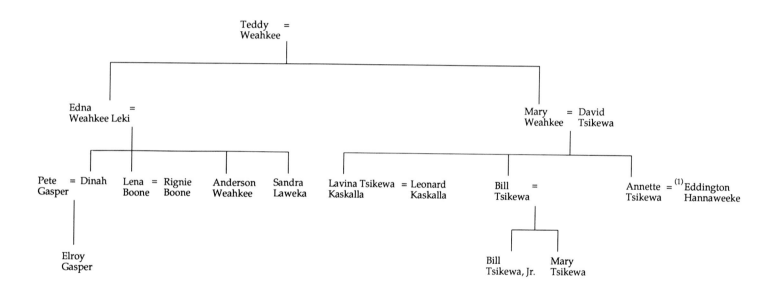

Teddy =
Weahkee

Edna =
Weahkee Leki

Pete = Dinah   Lena = Rignie   Anderson   Sandra
Gasper   Boone Boone   Weahkee   Laweka

Elroy
Gasper

Mary = David
Weahkee Tsikewa

Lavina Tsikewa = Leonard   Bill =   Annette = (1) Eddington
Kaskalla   Kaskalla   Tsikewa   Tsikewa   Hannaweeke

Bill   Mary
Tsikewa, Jr. Tsikewa

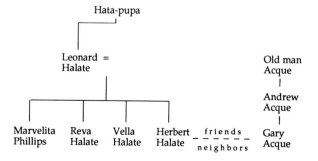

Hata-pupa

Leonard =
Halate

Marvelita   Reva   Vella   Herbert   friends   Old man
Phillips   Halate   Halate   Halate   ————————   Acque
                                        neighbors
                                                    Andrew
                                                    Acque

                                                    Gary
                                                    Acque

82

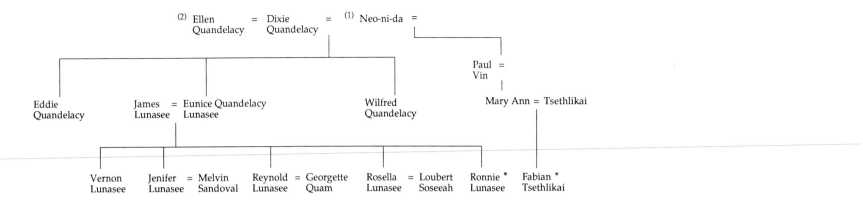

Fabian and Ronnie are related through Neo-ni-da.

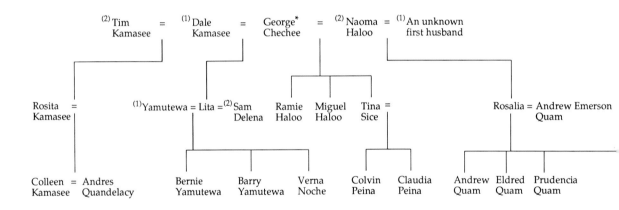

George Chechee influenced the work of his stepdaughter, Rosalia

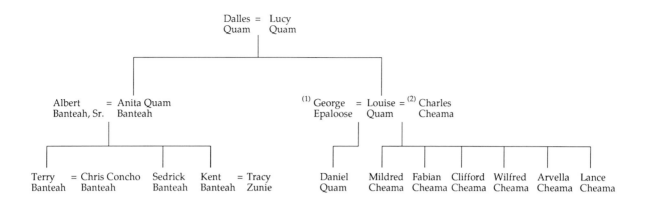

Dalles = Lucy
Quam   Quam

Albert   = Anita Quam   (1) George = Louise = (2) Charles
Banteah, Sr.   Banteah   Epaloose   Quam   Cheama

Terry   = Chris Concho   Sedrick   Kent   = Tracy   Daniel   Mildred   Fabian   Clifford   Wilfred   Arvella   Lance
Banteah   Banteah   Banteah   Banteah   Zunie   Quam   Cheama   Cheama   Cheama   Cheama   Cheama   Cheama

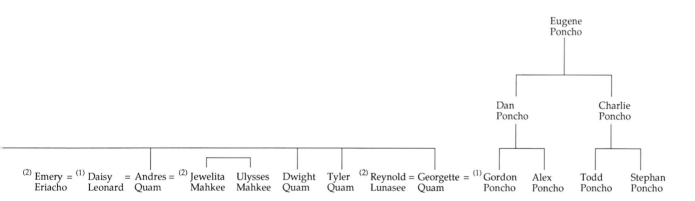

Eugene
Poncho

Dan   Charlie
Poncho   Poncho

(2) Emery = (1) Daisy = Andres = (2) Jewelita   Ulysses   Dwight   Tyler   (2) Reynold = Georgette = (1) Gordon   Alex   Todd   Stephan
Eriacho   Leonard   Quam   Mahkee   Mahkee   Quam   Quam   Lunasee   Quam   Poncho   Poncho   Poncho   Poncho

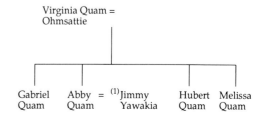

Virginia Quam =
Ohmsattie

Gabriel   Abby = (1) Jimmy   Hubert   Melissa
Quam   Quam   Yawakia   Quam   Quam

Adair, John
1944 *The Navajo and Pueblo Silversmiths.*
Norman: University of Oklahoma Press.

Branson, Oscar
1976 *Fetishes and Carvings of the Southwest.*
Phoenix: Treasure Chest Publications.

Bunzel, Ruth
1929 *The Pueblo Potter.* Reprint. New York:
Dover Press, 1972.

1929-30 *Zuni Katcinas.* Bureau of American
Ethnology. 47th Annual Report. Washington, D.C.

Cushing, Frank H.
1883 *Zuni Fetiches.* Bureau of American
Ethnology. 2nd Annual Report. Reprinted with
introduction by Tom Bahti. Flagstaff: KC
Publications, 1966.

Eggan, Fred and Pandey, T. N.
1983 "Zuni History, 1855-1970," In *Handbook of
the North American Indian*, pp.474-481. Vol. 9.
Alfonso Ortiz,Editor. Washington, D.C.
Smithsonian Institution.

Ferguson, T. J., and Hart, E. Richard
1985 *A Zuni Atlas.* Norman: University of
Oklahoma Press.

Figure 149. This modern photograph of the old dance plaza at Zuni shows little changes from the first view of it taken in 1879 by John Hillers.

Kintigh, Keith W.
1985 *Zuni Settlement Patterns.* Tucson: University of Arizona Press.

Kirk, Ruth
1943 "Zuni Fetishism," *El Palacio,* 50, pp. 6-10. Reprinted. Albuquerque: Avanyu Publishing Co. 1989.

Ladd, Edmund
1979 "Zuni Economy" in *Handbook of the North American Indian*, pp. 492-498. Vol. 9. Alfonso Ortiz, Editor. Washington, D.C.: Smithsonian Institution.

1983 "Zuni Social and Political Organization" in *Handbook of the North American Indian*, pp. 482-491. Vol. 9. Alfonso Ortiz, Editor. Washington, D.C.: Smithsonian Institution.

Sotheby-Parke Bernet, Inc.
Nov.14-16, 1975 *The C.G. Wallace Collection of American Indian Art.* Phoenix.

Stevenson, Matilda Coxe
1901-02 "The Zuni Indians." Bureau of American Ethnology. *23rd Annual Report.*

Tedlock, Dennis
1983 "Zuni Religion and World View" in *Handbook of the North American Indian,* pp. 499-508. Vol. 9. Alfonso Ortiz, Editor. Washington, D.C.: Smithsonian Institution.

Ukestine, Danny
1989 "Ancestral Homecoming" in *Experience Zuni, New Mexico*. p. 4. Zuni Area Chamber of Commerce,

Woodbury, Richard B.
1979 "Zuni Prehistory and History to 1850" in *Handbook of the North American Indian*, pp. 467-473. Vol. 9. Alfonso Ortiz, Editor. Washington, D.C.: Smithsonian Institution.

Wright, Barton (editor)
1988 *The Mythic World of the Zuni: As Written by Frank Hamilton Cushing*. Albuquerque: University of New Mexico Press.